The
Empty
Nesters
Cookbook

Rediscover Cooking for Two

FAMILY SERIES

Printed in the United States of America
by G&R Publishing Company

Distributed by:

CQ Products

507 Industrial Street
Waverly, IA 50677

ISBN-13: 978-1-56383-238-3
ISBN-10: 1-56383-238-0

Item #6224

Table of Contents

Beverages

Hot Apple Spiced Cider

⅓ orange peel

⅓ lemon peel

2 C. apple cider

1 T. plus 1 tsp. maple syrup

⅔ cinnamon stick

2 whole cloves

2 whole allspice berries

────────────── She does ──────────────

Cut the orange and lemon peel into strips.

────────────── He does ──────────────

In a large stainless steel saucepan, place the apple cider and maple syrup.

────────────── She does ──────────────

Place the orange peel, lemon peel, cinnamon stick, cloves and allspice berries in the center of a square of cheesecloth. Fold up the sides of the cheesecloth to enclose the bundle and tie with a length of kitchen string. Drop the spice bundle into the cider mixture.

────────────── He does ──────────────

Place the saucepan over medium heat for 5 to 10 minutes, or until the cider is very hot, but not boiling. Remove the cider from the heat and discard the spice bundle. Ladle the cider into big cups or mugs, adding a fresh cinnamon stick to each serving if desired.

Cappuccino Mix

1 C. powdered
   non-dairy creamer
1 C. instant chocolate
   drink mix

¾ C. instant coffee granules
½ C. sugar
½ tsp. cinnamon
¼ tsp. nutmeg

She does

In a medium bowl, combine the non-dairy creamer, instant chocolate drink mix, instant coffee granules, sugar, cinnamon and nutmeg. Mix well and transfer mixture to an air-tight container or glass jar with a tight-fitting lid.

He does

In a medium saucepan over medium heat, bring 1½ cups water to a boil. To prepare each serving, place 2 tablespoons of the drink mix in each mug. Add ¾ cup boiling water to each mug and stir until mixture is completely dissolved. Serve hot.

Citrus Spiced Tea Mix

1 (3 oz.) pkg. lemon flavored iced tea mix
2 (1¾ oz.) pkgs. orange flavored drink mix

1⅓ T. cinnamon
2 tsp. ground cloves

He does

In a large bowl, combine lemon flavored iced tea mix, orange flavored drink mix, cinnamon and ground cloves. Mix well and transfer mixture to an air-tight container or glass jar with a tight-fitting lid.

She does

In a medium saucepan over medium heat, bring 2 cups water to a boil. To prepare each serving, place 2 to 3 teaspoons drink mix in each mug. Add 1 cup boiling water to each mug and stir until mixture is completely dissolved. Serve hot.

Peppermint Cocoa

**1½ (1 oz.) squares
semi-sweet chocolate
4 small peppermint candies
2 C. milk**

**4 T. whipped topping,
divided
2 small peppermint
candy canes**

——————She does——————

Chop the semi-sweet chocolate and crush the peppermint candies.

—————— He does ——————

In a medium saucepan over medium heat, heat milk until hot, being careful not to boil. Whisk in the chopped chocolate and the crushed peppermint candy. Mix until chocolate and peppermint are completely melted and smooth. Pour hot cocoa into 4 mugs.

——————She does——————

Garnish each serving with 2 tablespoons whipped topping and serve with candy canes to use as stirring sticks.

Homemade Eggnog

1½ C. milk
2 T. sugar, divided
1½ tsp. instant
   coffee granules

⅛ tsp. salt
1 egg, separated
¼ tsp. vanilla
¼ tsp. nutmeg

He does

In a medium saucepan over medium low heat, combine the milk, 1 tablespoon sugar, instant coffee granules and salt.

She does

In a medium bowl, beat the egg yolk. Slowly stir about half of milk mixture into egg yolk and then return to hot mixture. Heat for about 2 minutes, being careful not to let mixture boil.

He does

In a medium mixing bowl, beat egg white, remaining 1 tablespoon sugar and vanilla at medium speed until soft peaks form.

She does

Pour milk mixture into 2 warm mugs and garnish each serving with half of the beaten mixture. Sprinkle each serving with a little nutmeg.

Ultra Fruit Smoothies

½ kiwi
½ banana
¼ C. blueberries
½ C. strawberries

½ C. ice cubes
¼ C. orange juice
½ (8 oz.) container
   peach yogurt

—————————— He does ——————————
Peel and slice the kiwi. Peel and chop the banana.

——————————She does——————————
In a blender, combine the kiwi slices, chopped banana, blueberries, strawberries, ice cubes, orange juice and peach yogurt. Process on high until blended and smooth. Pour smoothies into two tall glasses and serve.

Watermelon Slushies

½ miniature watermelon
5 ice cubes

½ tsp. honey

———————————**She does**———————————

Cube the miniature watermelon and remove any seeds.

———————————**He does**———————————

Place the ice cubes into a blender. Cover and pulse until ice is crushed. Add the cubed watermelon and blend for about 1 minute. Add the honey and process for about 10 seconds. Pour slushies into two tall glasses and serve.

Vegetables

Creamy Brussels Sprouts

1 (10 oz.) pkg. frozen
  Brussels sprouts
½ small onion
1 T. butter or margarine
1½ tsp. brown sugar
1 tsp. flour

¼ tsp. salt
¼ tsp. dry mustard
⅛ tsp. pepper
¼ C. milk
½ C. sour cream

He does

Fill a medium pot halfway with water. Bring to a boil over medium high heat. Place Brussels sprouts packet in boiling water. Boil for about 15 minutes, turning packet over after 10 minutes. Carefully remove packet from boiling water. Cut packet open and pour Brussels sprouts into a medium bowl. Once Brussels sprouts have cooled slightly, cut each sprout in half and set aside.

She does

Chop the small onion. In a medium skillet over medium heat, place butter. Add chopped onion and sauté until tender. Mix in brown sugar, flour, salt, dry mustard and pepper. Mix well and add milk. Heat until mixture is thick and bubbly.

He does

Place sour cream in a small bowl. Gradually add ¼ cup of the hot mixture to the sour cream. Mix well and slowly return sour cream mixture to saucepan. Add halved Brussels sprouts and stir gently. Cook until thoroughly heated, being careful not to boil. Serve immediately.

Sweet Dinner Carrots

3 large carrots
1 tsp. brown sugar
½ tsp. cornstarch

⅛ tsp. salt
3 T. orange juice
2 tsp. butter or margarine

He does

Fill a medium pot halfway with water. Bring to a boil over medium high heat. Slice the carrots and place sliced carrots in boiling water. Heat until tender, about 8 to 10 minutes. Drain carrots and place in a serving bowl.

She does

In a medium saucepan over low heat, combine brown sugar, cornstarch, salt, orange juice and butter. Heat, stirring occasionally, until mixture is thick and bubbly. Pour hot mixture over carrots in serving bowl and toss lightly until evenly coated. Serve immediately.

Baked Scalloped Corn

14 saltine crackers
1 T. butter or margarine,
  melted
½ small onion
1 egg, beaten

1 (14¾ oz.) can
  cream-style corn
3 T. milk
⅛ tsp. pepper

He does

Preheat oven to 350°. Crush the saltine crackers and divide in half. Place ½ of the crushed crackers in a small bowl and add the melted butter. Toss until well combined.

She does

Finely chop the small onion. In a medium bowl, combine chopped onion, beaten egg, cream-style corn, milk, pepper and remaining the crushed crackers. Mix until well combined and transfer mixture to a casserole dish.

He does

Sprinkle crushed cracker mixture over corn mixture and bake in oven for 30 minutes.

Broccoli in Cheese Sauce

1 (16 oz.) pkg. frozen
  broccoli spears
1 T. butter or margarine
1 T. flour
Pinch of salt

⅓ C. milk
3 T. shredded
  American cheese
3 T. shredded Swiss cheese

She does

Fill a medium pot halfway with water. Bring to a boil over medium high heat. Add the frozen broccoli spears to boiling water. Heat until tender, about 10 minutes. Drain broccoli and place in a serving bowl.

He does

In a medium saucepan over medium heat, melt butter. Blend in the flour and salt. Add milk and heat, stirring constantly, until thick and bubbly. Stir in shredded American cheese and shredded Swiss cheese. Heat, stirring constantly, until cheese is completely melted. Drizzle cheese sauce over cooked broccoli to serve.

Spam
Baked Beans

1 (12 oz.) can Spam   **2 T. brown sugar**
1 small onion   **2 T. molasses**
1 (11 oz.) can pork n' beans **1 T. prepared mustard**

───────────────── **He does** ─────────────────

Preheat oven to 375°. Cut Spam into 3 slices. Cut two thick slices from the onion.

───────────────── **She does** ─────────────────

In a small baking dish, combine pork n' beans, brown sugar, molasses and mustard. Top with Spam slices and then top with onion slices. Bake in oven for 35 to 40 minutes.

Cheesy Twice Baked Potatoes

2 large baking potatoes
¼ C. sour cream
¼ C. shredded
  Cheddar cheese
2 T. milk

¼ tsp. salt
Pinch of pepper
Pinch of paprika
1 T. grated Parmesan cheese
1 tsp. dried parsley flakes

He does

Preheat oven to 425°. Place baking potatoes in oven for 45 to 60 minutes, or until tender. Carefully remove potatoes from oven and cut a ⅜″ slice lengthwise from each potato. Remove skin from slice and place in a medium bowl. Scoop remaining insides from potato and place in same bowl. Reserve the potato shells and set aside.

She does

Using a potato masher, mash potato flesh in bowl and add sour cream, shredded Cheddar cheese, milk, salt, pepper and paprika. Beat until smooth. Mound potato filling into shells. Sprinkle Parmesan cheese and dried parsley flakes over filling. Place stuffed potatoes in a small baking dish and return to oven until thoroughly heated, about 25 to 30 minutes.

Vegetable Spanish Rice

1 small green pepper
1 small onion
1 small clove garlic
1 medium tomato
1 T. vegetable oil
⅔ C. cold water

½ C. long grain rice
¾ tsp. salt
½ tsp. chicken
    bouillon granules
Dash of hot pepper sauce

She does

Chop the green pepper and the onion.

He does

Mince the garlic. Peel and chop the tomato.

She does

In a large saucepan over medium high heat, place vegetable oil. Add chopped green pepper, chopped onion and minced garlic and sauté until vegetables are tender. Mix in cold water, long grain rice, chopped tomato, salt, chicken granules and hot pepper sauce. Mix until well combined and bring to a boil. Reduce heat, cover and let simmer for about 20 minutes, or until rice is tender and liquid has been absorbed.

Stuffed Red Peppers

¼ C. white rice, uncooked
¼ C. plus 2 T. water
2 large red bell peppers
½ onion, chopped
2 T. olive oil

1 T. fresh chopped parsley
1½ C. tomato sauce, divided
Salt and pepper to taste
¼ C. shredded
    mozzarella cheese

She does

Preheat oven to 400°. In a small saucepan, combine rice and water. Bring to a boil, reduce heat to low, and let simmer for about 15 minutes.

He does

Cut tops off of red peppers and scoop out seeds from inside. Arrange peppers in a large baking dish. Chop removed tops of peppers and place in a large skillet over medium heat. Add olive oil and chopped onion and sauté until vegetables are softened. Stir in fresh chopped parsley. Reduce heat to low and continue cooking for 5 minutes.

She does

Mix cooked rice and 1 cup tomato sauce into saucepan and season with salt and pepper to taste. Spoon mixture into hollowed peppers in baking dish and top each pepper with some of the remaining tomato sauce. Cover baking dish with aluminum foil and place in oven for about 45 minutes.

He does

Uncover baking dish and top each pepper with mozzarella cheese. Return to oven for a few minutes, until cheese is melted.

Easy Oven Potatoes

1 small green bell pepper	2 tsp. vegetable oil
1 small onion	¼ tsp. dried rosemary
2 medium potatoes	¼ tsp. dried thyme
2 cloves garlic	2 T. lemon juice

He does

Preheat oven to 450°. Cut two pieces of aluminum foil to about 12 x 15″ and set aside. Thinly slice the green bell pepper and onion.

She does

Thoroughly scrub the potatoes. Cut the potatoes into very thin slices. Mince the garlic.

He does

In a large bowl, toss together the potato slices, onion slices, green bell pepper slices, minced garlic, vegetable oil, rosemary and thyme. Toss until well combined and divide mixture evenly onto the aluminum foil pieces.

She does

Drizzle lemon juice over potato mixture. Fold up aluminum foil to securely, but loosely, form a flat package. Place packets, seam side up, on baking sheets. Bake in oven for about 20 minutes, or until potatoes are tender.

Seasoned Red Onion Rings

2 C. frying oil
1 large red onion
¼ C. seasoned salt

1½ C. flour
Salt to taste

———————————— She does ————————————

In a heavy large skillet over high heat, heat oil to 365°.

———————————— He does ————————————

Slice the onion into ½″ slices and separate slices into rings. Place the onion rings in a large bag or bowl.

———————————— She does ————————————

In a medium bowl, combine seasoned salt and flour. Add flour mixture to onion rings and toss until lightly coated.

———————————— He does ————————————

Place a few coated onions at a time into the hot oil and fry until batter is light golden brown. Remove onion rings to paper towels to drain and repeat with remaining rings. Season with salt to taste.

Asparagus & Water Chestnuts

½ small red onion
1 (8 oz.) can sliced
  water chestnuts
1 (15 oz.) can
  asparagus spears

1 tsp. olive oil
1 tsp. balsamic vinegar

She does

Dice the red onion. Drain the water chestnuts and asparagus.

He does

In a medium skillet over medium high heat, place the olive oil. Add the diced red onion and sauté until lightly softened. Stir in drained water chestnuts, drained asparagus spears and balsamic vinegar. Heat, stirring occasionally, until the asparagus is tender, about 10 minutes.

Blended
Spring Vegetables

6 to 8 asparagus spears
2 large carrots
20 fresh snow peas
2 green onions
1½ tsp. butter or margarine

¼ C. frozen pearl onions
½ tsp. salt
½ C. water
¼ C. frozen peas
Salt and pepper to taste

She does

Cut the asparagus into 1″ pieces. Peel and cut the carrots into ¼″ thick slices.

He does

Trim the snow peas and chop the green onions.

She does

In a large deep saucepan over medium high heat, melt butter. Slowly add frozen pearl onions and sauté until onions are softened and golden brown, about 5 minutes. Remove saucepan from heat.

He does

Add asparagus pieces, sliced carrots, trimmed snow peas, salt and water to saucepan. Return to high heat, cover and cook until vegetables start to steam. Let vegetables steam, covered, until almost tender, about 5 minutes. Stir in frozen peas and continue to steam until vegetables are just tender, about 1 minute. Stir in chopped green onions and season with additional salt and pepper to taste. Serve immediately.

Sweet
Vegetable Medley

½ lb. baby carrots

½ lb. Brussels sprouts

¼ C. plus 2 T. chicken broth

1½ T. butter or margarine

1½ T. brown sugar

¾ tsp. pepper

She does

Fill a medium pot halfway with water. Bring to a boil over medium high heat. Add the baby carrots to boiling water. Heat until tender but still crisp, about 4 minutes. Remove carrots with a slotted spoon and immediately transfer cooked carrots to a bowl of ice water.

He does

Return water in pot to a boil. Add Brussels sprouts and cook until tender but crisp, about 5 minutes. Again, remove Brussels sprouts with a slotted spoon and immediately transfer to a bowl of ice water.

She does

In a large heavy skillet over medium high heat, combine chicken broth, butter and brown sugar. Bring to a boil, stirring constantly, until brown sugar completely dissolves. Continue to boil until mixture has reduced by half, about 7 minutes.

He does

Drain the carrots and Brussels sprouts. Add drained carrots to skillet and heat until almost tender, about 6 minutes, stirring to coat carrots in sauce. Add drained Brussels sprouts and pepper. Cook until thoroughly heated, about 4 minutes, stirring occasionally. Serve immediately.

Bacon & Green Pepper Fried Corn

2 ears corn
½ small green bell pepper

2 slices bacon

He does

Husk and clean the ears of corn. Slice corn from the cobs and set aside.

She does

Chop the green bell pepper.

He does

In a large skillet over medium high heat, cook bacon until evenly brown. Remove from skillet and set on paper towels to drain. Crumble the bacon.

She does

Add chopped green pepper to bacon grease in skillet and sauté until softened. Add the corn and continue to heat until corn is tender. Stir in the crumbled bacon and cook for an additional 1 minute, or until thoroughly heated. Serve immediately.

Oregano Baked Sweet Potatoes

1 T. olive oil
1 large sweet potato
2 tsp. dried oregano

1 tsp. salt
1 tsp. pepper

————————She does————————

Preheat oven to 350°. Coat the bottom of an 8″ square glass baking dish with olive oil.

———————— He does ————————

Wash and peel the sweet potato. Cut the sweet potato into 2″ cubes. Place cubed sweet potato in baking dish and turn to coat in the olive oil. Sprinkle oregano, salt and pepper over sweet potato and gently toss until evenly combined. Bake in oven for 30 minutes or until sweet potatoes are softened.

Salads

Cooked Cabbage Cole Slaw

½ small onion
1 slice bacon
1 T. white vinegar
1 T. water
2 tsp. sugar

¼ tsp. salt
⅛ tsp. pepper
2 C. shredded cabbage
¼ C. shredded carrot
¼ C. creamy salad dressing

He does

Chop the small onion.

She does

In a large skillet over medium high heat, cook bacon until crisp. Remove from skillet and set on paper towels to drain. Crumble the bacon and set aside.

He does

Add chopped onion to bacon drippings in skillet and sauté over medium high heat until onions are tender. Stir in white vinegar, water, sugar, salt and pepper. Bring just to boiling and stir in shredded cabbage and shredded carrots. Toss until evenly coated, cover and heat for an additional 5 minutes.

She does

Stir in creamy salad dressing and top with crumbled bacon. Serve immediately.

Dill Potato Salad

¼ tsp. mustard seed
¼ tsp. dillweed
1 T. water
2 large potatoes
1 green onion

1 stalk celery
1 hard-boiled egg
½ tsp. salt
¼ C. creamy salad dressing

She does

In a large bowl, soak mustard seed and dillweed in 1 tablespoon water overnight.

He does

Place the potatoes in a large pot of boiling water. Boil until potatoes are tender, about 25 minutes. Carefully remove potatoes from water and let cool slightly. If desired, peel the potatoes. Chop the potatoes into 1″ pieces.

She does

Dice the green onion and celery.

He does

Peel and chop the hard-boiled egg.

She does

Stir salt into the water and seed mixture. Add the chopped potatoes, diced green onion, diced celery, chopped hard-boiled egg and creamy salad dressing. Toss until evenly coated and chill in refrigerator until ready to serve.

Macaroni Salad

1 C. elbow macaroni,
  uncooked
1 hard-boiled egg
½ small onion
3 T. mayonnaise
1 tsp. white vinegar

1 tsp. sugar
¼ tsp. salt
¼ tsp. prepared mustard
Pepper to taste

She does

    Fill a large pot with lightly salted water and bring to a boil. Add elbow macaroni and cook for 8 to 10 minutes, or until pasta is al dente. Drain pasta and set aside.

He does

    Peel and chop the hard-boiled egg.

She does

    Chop the onion.

He does

    In a medium bowl, combine drained macaroni, chopped hard-boiled egg, chopped onion, mayonnaise, white vinegar, sugar, salt, prepared mustard and pepper. Toss until evenly coated and chill in refrigerator at least 1 hour before serving.

Taco Salad for Two

½ lb. ground beef
1 (10 oz.) can diced tomatoes
2 green onions
6 pitted ripe olives
1 C. corn chips
2 C. torn lettuce leaves

½ C. shredded sharp
  Cheddar cheese
1 (16 oz.) can spicy
  refried beans
1 tsp. chili powder
¼ tsp. salt

——————————She does——————————

In a large skillet over medium high heat, brown the ground beef and drain off fat. Drain the diced tomatoes, reserving the liquid.

——————————He does——————————

Chop the green onions and slice the olives.

——————————She does——————————

Crush the corn chips.

——————————He does——————————

In a salad bowl, combine lettuce leaves, shredded cheese, chopped green onions and sliced olives. Toss well and sprinkle drained tomatoes and crushed corn chips over top.

——————————She does——————————

To meat in skillet, stir in reserved tomato liquid, refried beans, chili powder and salt. Bring to a boil. Pour over lettuce mixture and toss until well incorporated. Serve immediately.

Seasoned Green Bean Salad

1 (14½ oz.) can green beans
½ small onion
1 medium tomato

¼ C. sour cream
3 T. Italian dressing

He does

Drain the green beans and chop the small onion.

She does

Peel and chop the tomato.

He does

In a medium bowl, combine the sour cream and Italian dressing. Stir in the drained green beans, chopped onion and chopped tomato. Mix until well combined. Chill in refrigerator at least 2 hours before serving.

Peppered Cooked Spinach Salad

1 T. butter
1 slice bacon
1 green onion
4 C. fresh spinach leaves
1 tsp. prepared mustard

2 tsp. sugar
¼ C. white wine vinegar
1 oz. brandy
1 hard-boiled egg
Pepper to taste

He does

In a medium skillet over medium high heat, melt butter. Dice the bacon. Add diced bacon to skillet and heat until crisp. Chop the green onion and add to skillet.

She does

Place fresh spinach leaves in a medium bowl.

He does

In a small bowl, whisk together prepared mustard, sugar and white wine vinegar. Mix well and add to skillet. Let mixture simmer, stirring occasionally, until very hot. Add brandy and carefully light mixture with a match, and flame for 5 seconds.

She does

Invert skillet over salad bowl, allowing spinach to steam slightly. Remove skillet and toss spinach and ingredients together.

He does

Peel the hard-boiled egg and remove the cooked yolk. Chop the white part only and sprinkle over salad. Season with pepper and serve immediately.

Raisin & Almond Broccoli Salad

2 slices bacon
½ head fresh broccoli
½ small red onion
3 T. raisins

3 T. slivered almonds
¼ C. mayonnaise
1 T. sugar
1¼ tsp. white wine vinegar

She does

In a large skillet over medium high heat, cook bacon until crisp. Remove from skillet and set on paper towels to drain. Crumble the bacon.

He does

Chop the broccoli into bite-sized pieces. Thinly chop the red onion.

She does

In a medium bowl, combine broccoli pieces, red onion slices, crumbled bacon, raisins and slivered almonds.

He does

In a medium bowl, whisk together mayonnaise, sugar and white wine vinegar, mixing until smooth. Pour over ingredients in salad bowl and toss until evenly incorporated. Chill in refrigerator until ready to serve.

Twisted Carrot Salad

1 large carrot
1 stalk celery
⅓ C. raisins
⅓ C. chopped walnuts
2 tsp. shredded coconut

2 T. plus 2 tsp. mayonnaise
2 tsp. sour cream
1 tsp. apple cider vinegar
⅛ tsp. sugar
⅛ tsp. salt

—————————She does—————————

Shred the carrot.

————————— He does —————————

Finely chop the celery.

—————————She does—————————

In a medium bowl, combine shredded carrots, chopped celery, raisins, chopped walnuts and shredded coconut.

————————— He does —————————

In a small bowl, whisk together mayonnaise, sour cream, vinegar, sugar and salt. Pour dressing over carrot mixture and toss until evenly incorporated. Chill in refrigerator until ready to serve.

B.L.T. Salad

4 slices bacon
¼ C. mayonnaise
1 T. red wine vinegar
1 T. dried basil
2 slices French bread

½ tsp. salt
½ tsp. pepper
1½ tsp. vegetable oil
½ lb. romaine lettuce
8 cherry tomatoes

She does

In a large skillet over medium high heat, cook bacon until crisp. Remove bacon from skillet and reserve 2 tablespoons bacon drippings. Set bacon on paper towels to drain. Crumble the bacon.

He does

In a small bowl, whisk together the reserved bacon drippings, mayonnaise, red wine vinegar and dried basil. Mix well, cover and let stand at room temperature.

She does

Cut the French bread slices into ½″ pieces. In a medium skillet over medium heat, toss the bread pieces with the salt and pepper. Drizzle vegetable oil over bread and continue tossing until bread pieces are golden brown.

He does

Tear the romaine lettuce into small pieces and quarter the cherry tomatoes.

She does

In a large bowl, toss together romaine lettuce, quartered tomatoes, crumbled bacon and bread cubes. Pour dressing over the salad and toss until well incorporated. Serve immediately.

Apple Cabbage Slaw

¼ C. plain yogurt
2 T. sour cream
1 tsp. honey
½ small head red cabbage

½ small onion
1 Granny Smith apple
1 T. dried parsley flakes
Salt and pepper to taste

She does

In a medium bowl, whisk together the plain yogurt, sour cream and honey, blending until smooth. Place in refrigerator until chilled.

He does

Shred the red cabbage. Mince the small onion.

She does

Peel, core and chop the apple.

He does

Add shredded cabbage, minced onion, chopped apples and dried parsley flakes to dressing mixture. Season with salt and pepper to taste and toss until evenly incorporated.

She does

Chill in refrigerator until ready to serve.

Summer Garden Tomato Salad

2 large tomatoes
1 small cucumber
1 clove garlic
½ red onion
½ yellow onion
½ head romaine lettuce

¼ C. olive oil
1 T. red wine vinegar
¼ tsp. sugar
½ tsp. dried oregano
Salt and pepper to taste

He does

Cut the tomatoes into wedges. Peel and dice the cucumber. Mince the garlic.

She does

Cut the red onion and the yellow onion into wedges and separate the pieces. Tear the romaine lettuce into small pieces.

He does

In a large bowl, combine tomato wedges, diced cucumber, red onion pieces and yellow onion pieces.

She does

In a medium bowl, whisk together the minced garlic, olive oil, red wine vinegar, sugar, dried oregano, salt and pepper. Pour dressing over tomato mixture and toss to coat evenly. Cover and chill in refrigerator until ready to serve.

Spicy Tomato & Apple Salad

½ chile pepper
1 large tomato
1 medium apple
¾ tsp. salt

½ tsp. sugar
½ tsp. soy sauce
Juice of ½ lemon
½ C. chopped peanuts

She does

Chop the chile pepper and remove the seeds. Cut the tomato into thin slices.

He does

Peel, core and slice the apple.

She does

In a medium bowl, toss together the chopped chile pepper, salt, sugar and soy sauce. Squeeze the juice from the lemon over ingredients. Add the tomato and apple slices and toss until evenly coated.

He does

Sprinkle the chopped peanuts over salad and chill in refrigerator until ready to serve

Shrimp n' Angel Hair Pasta Salad

⅔ (8 oz.) pkg. angel
   hair pasta
1 T. olive oil

10 to 12 medium shrimp
4 green onions
½ C. ranch dressing

He does

Fill a large pot with lightly salted water and bring to a boil. Add angel hair pasta and cook for 8 to 10 minutes, or until pasta is al dente. Drain pasta and set aside.

She does

In a medium saucepan over medium heat, place olive oil. Once oil is hot, add shrimp to saucepan and cook, stirring occasionally, until shrimp are thoroughly cooked, about 2 minutes.

He does

Chop the green onions.

She does

In a large bowl, toss together drained pasta, cooked shrimp, chopped green onions and ranch dressing. Mix until evenly incorporated. Serve immediately or chill in refrigerator overnight.

Simple Cheddar Pea Salad

1 (8 oz.) can peas
2 oz. Cheddar cheese
½ small sweet onion

1½ tsp. sugar
2 T. creamy salad dressing

———————— **He does** ————————

Drain the peas and cut the Cheddar cheese into cubes.

———————— **She does** ————————

Finely chop the onion.

———————— **He does** ————————

In a medium bowl, toss together the drained peas, Cheddar cheese cubes and chopped onion. Stir in the sugar and creamy salad dressing. Toss until evenly incorporated and chill in refrigerator at least 1 hour before serving.

Chicken Salad

1 T. butter or margarine
1 chicken breast
1 hard-boiled egg
1 stalk celery

½ tsp. prepared mustard
⅓ C. mayonnaise
½ tsp. lemon juice

He does

In a medium skillet over medium high heat, place the butter. Add the chicken breast and heat until thoroughly cooked, turning once. Remove chicken from skillet and cut into small pieces.

She does

Peel and chop the hard-boiled egg and chop the celery.

He does

In a medium bowl, combine cooked chicken pieces, chopped egg and chopped celery. Mix in the mustard, mayonnaise and lemon juice. Toss until evenly coated and season with salt and pepper to taste. Chill in refrigerator until ready to serve.

Ham Salad in Pineapple Shells

1 small pineapple, chilled
½ small green bell pepper
2 oz. cooked ham

1 stalk celery
⅓ C. mayonnaise
½ tsp. mustard

She does
Cut pineapple in half lengthwise. Remove core. Cut pineapple fruit from shell to within ½″ from the edge, reserving the shell. Chop the pineapple into small pieces.

He does
Chop the green pepper. Chop the cooked ham into pieces. Dice the celery.

She does
In a medium bowl, combine chopped pineapple, chopped green pepper, chopped ham and diced celery. Stir in mayonnaise and mustard, mixing until evenly incorporated. To serve, spoon ham salad into hollowed pineapple shells.

Curried Apple Salad

4 baking apples
½ C. sugar
½ C. butter

Juice of ½ lemon
½ tsp. curry powder

He does

Preheat oven to 325°. Peel, core and quarter the apples. Place quartered apples in an 8″ square baking dish.

She does

In a medium bowl, cream together the sugar and butter. Mix in juice from the lemon and curry powder. Sprinkle mixture over apples and bake in oven for 20 to 30 minutes, or until apples are tender. Excellent when served with cooked ham, pork or corned beef.

Soups & Sandwiches

Red Pepper Legume Soup

1 onion
1 large clove garlic
1 large carrot
1 leek
1 green onion
1 small red bell pepper
½ bunch watercress
1½ T. butter

1 (14½ oz.) can chicken broth
2¼ C. water
½ (10 oz.) bag fresh spinach
1 T. salt
Pepper to taste
1 T. red wine vinegar
1 (8 oz.) can peas, drained

She does

Chop the onion and mince the garlic. Peel and chop the carrot.

He does

Chop only the bulb part of the leek and only the stem of the green onion. Cut the red bell pepper into thin strips. Trim and chop the watercress.

She does

In a large saucepan over medium high heat, melt the butter. Add the chopped onion and minced garlic and sauté until vegetables are tender, about 5 minutes. Stir in the chicken broth, water, fresh spinach, chopped carrots, chopped leek, chopped green onion, red bell pepper strips and trimmed watercress. Bring mixture to a boil, reduce heat and let simmer for 30 minutes, or until carrots are tender. Season with salt and pepper to taste and drizzle red wine vinegar over top. Add drained peas and heat, stirring occasionally, for an additional 5 minutes.

Simple Tomato Bisque

1 (10¾ oz.) can tomato soup   **1 (3 oz.) pkg. cream cheese**
1¼ C. water

—————————————— **He does** ——————————————

In a medium saucepan over medium heat, combine tomato soup and water. Cook, stirring occasionally, until soup is thoroughly heated.

—————————————— **She does** ——————————————

Cut cream cheese into small pieces. Add cream cheese to soup and continue to heat, stirring occasionally, until cream cheese is completely melted. Season with pepper to taste. Serve immediately.

Creamy
Broccoli Soup

¾ C. plus 2 tsp.
  chicken broth
½ head broccoli
½ small onion
2½ tsp. flour

⅓ C. milk
⅓ C. shredded Cheddar
  cheese, optional
¼ tsp. dried oregano
Salt and pepper to taste

She does

In a large pot over medium high heat, place chicken broth. Bring mixture to a boil.

He does

Chop the broccoli and the onion.

She does

Add chopped broccoli and chopped onion to boiling broth. Heat for about 5 minutes, or until broccoli is tender.

He does

In a medium bowl, place flour. Slowly add milk to flour mixture and stir until well blended. Stir flour mixture back into soup pot and continue to heat until soup is thick and bubbly. If desired, stir in Cheddar cheese, mixing until cheese is completely melted. Stir in dried oregano and season with salt and pepper to taste. Ladle soup into bowls and serve immediately.

Italian
Chicken Chowder

¼ C. Italian dressing
1 boneless, skinless
  chicken breast
1 medium zucchini
1 (14½ oz.) can stewed
  tomatoes in juice

1 C. chicken broth
½ C. elbow macaroni,
  uncooked
1 tsp. dried basil
¼ C. shredded
  mozzarella cheese

She does

In a large saucepan over medium heat, place Italian dressing. Cook until dressing is heated. Chop the chicken breast into small pieces and add chopped chicken to dressing in skillet. Heat for about 3 minutes, stirring occasionally.

He does

Chop the zucchini. Stir chopped zucchini, stewed tomatoes in juice, chicken broth, uncooked macaroni and dried basil into ingredients in saucepan. Increase heat to high and bring to a boil. Reduce heat and let simmer for about 8 minutes, or until macaroni is tender and chicken is thoroughly cooked. Ladle soup into bowl and sprinkle shredded mozzarella cheese over top. Serve immediately.

Easy Chicken n' Rice Soup

1 (10¾ oz.) can cream
  of chicken soup
1 C. water

¾ C. instant white rice,
  uncooked

She does

In a medium saucepan over medium heat, combine cream of chicken soup and water. Cook, stirring occasionally, until soup is thoroughly heated.

He does

Bring mixture to a boil and stir in uncooked instant white rice. Remove from heat, cover and let stand for 5 minutes, or until rice is tender. Stir lightly and serve.

Creamy Mushroom Potato Soup

1 large potato
1 medium onion
1 (13¼ oz.) can mushroom
  stems and pieces

1 C. milk
Pinch of dried parsley flakes
Salt and pepper to taste

----------- He does -----------

Thoroughly scrub the potato and cut into cubes. Chop the onion.

----------- She does -----------

In a large saucepan over medium high heat, melt the butter. Add cubed potato and chopped onion. Sauté until potatoes are almost tender. Add can of mushrooms with juice and continue to cook until thoroughly heated.

----------- He does -----------

In a separate large saucepan over medium heat, place milk. Cook until milk is thoroughly heated, being careful not to boil. Add the potato mixture and stir until well combined. Continue to heat until soup reaches desired consistency. The soup will thicken the longer it is heated. Season with salt and pepper to taste.

French Onion Soup

2 onions
2½ C. plus 2 T. vegetable broth, divided
⅛ tsp. sugar
1 T. flour
¼ C. dry white wine
1 bay leaf

¼ tsp. dried thyme
¼ tsp. pepper
1½ tsp. brandy
1 clove garlic
2 slices French bread
3⅓ C. grated Parmesan cheese

He does

Cut the onions into thin slices.

She does

In a large saucepan over medium high heat, heat ¼ cup vegetable broth. Stir in the onion slices and continue to heat until onions are golden, about 15 minutes. Stir in the sugar and flour. Pour in the remaining vegetable broth and dry white wine.

He does

Add bay leaf, dried thyme and pepper. Bring soup to a boil for 8 minutes, stirring constantly. Reduce heat, partly cover and let simmer for 30 minutes. Remove soup from heat, remove bay leaf and stir in brandy.

She does

Preheat oven broiler. Toast the French bread slices. Cut the garlic clove in half and rub garlic over toasted bread slices.

He does

Ladle the soup into 2 ovenproof bowls and float one piece of toast on top of each bowl. Sprinkle grated Parmesan cheese over toast and place bowls under broiler for about 1 minute, or until cheese is melted.

Roasted Garlic Soup

2 bulbs garlic
2 T. olive oil
2 leeks
1 small onion
3 T. butter
3 T. flour
2 C. chicken broth

2 T. plus 2 tsp. dry sherry
½ C. heavy whipping cream
1½ tsp. lemon juice
Salt to taste
⅛ tsp. white pepper
1 green onion

He does

Preheat oven to 350°. Cut the top ¼″ off each garlic head. Place garlic bulbs in a small baking dish and drizzle olive oil over garlic. Bake in oven until golden, about 1 hour. Remove from oven and let cool slightly. Separate garlic bulbs into individual cloves. Press the cloves between thumb and finger to release from outer skin. Mince the garlic.

She does

Chop the leeks and onion. In a large saucepan over medium heat, melt the butter. Stir in the minced garlic, chopped leeks and chopped onion. Sauté vegetables for about 8 minutes, or until onions are translucent. Mix in flour and heat for about 10 minutes, stirring occasionally. Stir in chicken broth and dry sherry and let simmer for about 20 minutes, stirring occasionally. Remove from heat and let cool slightly.

He does

In a blender, puree soup mixture in batches and return to saucepan. Mix in heavy cream and let simmer about 10 minutes, or until soup has thickened. Mix in lemon juice and season with salt and white pepper. Ladle soup into bowls.

She does

Chop the green onion and sprinkle over each serving.

Slow Cooker
Ham Bone Soup

1 small onion
1 large potato
1 small green bell pepper
1 ham bone
1 (10 oz.) can diced
   tomatoes, drained

1 (15 oz.) can kidney
   beans, drained
3 cubes chicken bouillon
3 C. water

She does

Dice the onion and cube the potato.

He does

Chop the green bell pepper.

She does

In a slow cooker, place the diced onion, cubed potato, chopped green bell pepper, ham bone, drained tomatoes and drained kidney beans.

He does

In a small bowl, dissolve the chicken bouillon cubes in the water. Pour over ingredients in slow cooker. Cover and cook on high until warmed. Reduce heat to low and cook for 5 to 6 hours. Before serving, strip any remaining meat from the ham bone and add to soup. Discard the bone.

Chicken Veggie Soup

1 C. baby carrots
1 medium potato
1 (4 oz.) can mushrooms

1 (14½ oz.) can chicken broth
½ tsp. dried cilantro

―――――――――― **He does** ――――――――――

Cut the baby carrots in half.

―――――――――― **She does** ――――――――――

Peel and cube the potato. Drain the mushrooms.

―――――――――― **He does** ――――――――――

    In a large saucepan over medium high heat, combine the chicken broth, halved carrots and cubed potatoes. Let mixture simmer for about 20 minutes, or until potatoes are tender. Stir in the drained mushrooms and let simmer for an additional 5 minutes. Season with cilantro and ladle soup into bowls.

Fresh Vegetable Cheese Soup

½ small onion
½ small bunch broccoli
¼ small bunch cauliflower
2 large carrots
¼ C. butter or margarine
1¼ C. water
1½ tsp. chicken
  bouillon granules

2 T. flour
1 C. half n' half
1 C. shredded
  Cheddar cheese
Pepper to taste
Croutons, optional

She does

Chop the onion, broccoli, cauliflower and carrots.

He does

In a large soup pot over medium heat, melt the butter. Add the chopped onions and sauté until onions are tender. Add water and chicken bouillon granules. Bring mixture to a boil.

She does

Place flour in a separate bowl. Add some of the hot broth mixture to the flour and whisk together. Slowly add flour mixture back into soup. Stir in chopped broccoli, chopped cauliflower and chopped carrots. Let mixture simmer until vegetables are tender.

He does

Stir in half n' half and shredded Cheddar cheese. Season with pepper to taste. Continue to heat until cheese is melted, being careful not to boil. Ladle soup into bowls and, if desired, sprinkle croutons over each serving.

Potato Dumpling Soup

1 small yellow onion
3 potatoes
4 C. water
1½ tsp. butter
½ bay leaf
1 tsp. dried parsley flakes

Salt and pepper to taste
½ C. flour
1 egg
½ tsp. salt
¼ C. half n' half

He does

Quarter the onion and separate into individual pieces.

She does

Thoroughly scrub the potatoes and cut into cubes.

He does

In a large saucepan over medium high heat, combine the onion pieces, cubed potatoes, water, butter, bay leaf, dried parsley flakes, salt and pepper. Mix lightly and bring mixture to a boil.

She does

In a medium bowl, combine flour, egg and salt. Mix well and add a little water until a thick dough forms. Pinch off little pieces of the dough and roll lightly between your fingers. Once potatoes are tender, drop the dumplings into the hot soup. Once the dough pieces are fluffy, slowly add half n' half to soup. Cook until thoroughly heated, being careful not to boil. Ladle soup into bowls and serve immediately.

Jalapeno Cheese Soup

2 stalks celery
1 small onion
2 jalapeno peppers
2 C. chicken broth

¼ tsp. garlic salt
1 (12 oz.) bag shredded
  Cheddar cheese

He does

Chop the celery and onion.

She does

Dice the jalapeno peppers, discarding the seeds.

He does

In a large saucepan over high heat, combine chopped celery, chopped onion, chicken broth and garlic salt. Heat for about 10 minutes, or until mixture thickens, stirring occasionally. Remove from heat and stir in the shredded Cheddar cheese, mixing until cheese is melted.

She does

Transfer soup mixture to a blender and puree until soup is smooth. Return pureed mixture to pot and place over medium heat. Stir in chopped jalapenos and continue to cook until thoroughly heated. Ladle soup into bowls and serve immediately.

Cream of
Celery Soup

¾ C. chicken broth
3 stalks celery
1 large carrot
1 small onion
¾ C. milk

1 T. flour
⅛ tsp. salt
⅛ tsp. white pepper
1 T. margarine

─────────────── He does ───────────────

In a large pot over medium high heat, place chicken broth. Bring mixture to a boil. In the meantime, coarsely chop the celery.

─────────────── She does ───────────────

Slice the carrots into thin strips and chop the onion.

─────────────── He does ───────────────

Add chopped celery, carrot slices and chopped onion to boiling broth.

─────────────── She does ───────────────

Place milk in a large glass measuring cup. Heat in microwave for 30 seconds. Whisk flour, salt and white pepper into hot milk. Add milk mixture and margarine to pot and return to a boil for 10 minutes. Before serving, strain soup into bowls through a fine-holed sieve or colander, removing the vegetable pieces.

Shaved Roast Beef Sandwiches

1 T. Italian dressing
1 T. water
12 slices thinly shaved
   roast beef

2 hamburger buns, split
1 T. grated Parmesan cheese

----------------- He does -----------------

In a medium microwave-safe bowl, combine Italian dressing and water. Add thinly sliced roast beef and toss lightly. Cover bowl with plastic wrap, poking a few holes in plastic for ventilation. Heat in microwave on high setting for 45 seconds, or until roast beef is heated throughout.

----------------- She does -----------------

Remove from microwave and stir lightly. Pile shaved roast beef on bottom half of buns and sprinkle grated Parmesan cheese over each sandwich. Cover with tops of buns and serve.

Super Subs

2 French rolls
3 T. butter
2 tsp. mustard
2 slices bologna
2 slices cooked ham

4 slices salami
¼ C. shredded
   Cheddar cheese
½ C. shredded lettuce

She does

Preheat oven to 450°. Split French rolls in half. In a small bowl, combine butter and mustard. Spread mixture over inside of each French roll half.

He does

Arrange 1 slice bologna, 1 slice cooked ham and 2 slices salami on each roll. Top each sandwich with an even amount of shredded Cheddar cheese and shredded lettuce. Place other roll half on each sandwich.

She does

Wrap each sub in aluminum foil and place on top oven rack for about 20 minutes.

Dijon Grilled Ham & Cheese

1 tomato
2 T. butter
4 slices whole wheat bread
2 tsp. Dijon mustard

2 slices salami
2 slices Swiss cheese
4 slices ham

He does

Cut 2 thin slices from the tomato.

She does

Spread butter over 1 side of each bread slice. Spread mustard over the other side of two of the bread slices. Place 1 slice salami, 1 tomato slice, 1 Swiss cheese slice and 2 ham slices over bread slices with mustard. Top with remaining bread slices, buttered side up.

He does

Place sandwiches a large skillet over medium heat. Heat until cheese is melted and bread is lightly toasted on one side. Flip sandwiches over and heat until remaining side is toasted.

Spicy Cheddar Tuna Melts

1 Serrano pepper
1 (6 oz.) can tuna in water
2 oz. Cheddar cheese
1 plum tomato
½ C. mayonnaise

1½ tsp. dried dillweed
1½ tsp. sweet relish
¼ tsp. seasoned salt
4 slices bread

He does

Chop the Serrano pepper, discarding the seeds. Drain the tuna.

She does

Cut the Cheddar cheese into 4 slices. Cut the tomato into thin slices.

He does

In medium bowl, combine the chopped pepper, drained tuna, mayonnaise, dried dillweed, sweet relish and seasoned salt. Mix until well combined.

She does

Preheat oven broiler. Place an even amount of the tuna salad over two slices of bread. Place two Cheddar cheese slices over each sandwich. Place under broiler until cheese is melted, about 1 to 2 minutes. Carefully remove sandwiches from oven and place half of the tomato slices over each sandwich. Top with remaining slices of bread and return to broiler until bread is toasted, about 1 minute.

Dill Egg Salad Sandwiches

¼ small red onion
4 eggs
1½ tsp. mayonnaise
1 T. Dijon mustard
½ tsp. dried dillweed

½ tsp. paprika
Salt and pepper to taste
2 large lettuce leaves
4 bread slices

───────── **He does** ─────────

Mince the red onion.

───────── **She does** ─────────

Place eggs in a medium saucepan and cover with cold water. Place over medium high heat and bring water to a boil. Remove saucepan from heat, cover, and let eggs stand in water for 10 to 12 minutes. Remove eggs from hot water and run under cool water. Peel and chop the hard-boiled eggs.

───────── **He does** ─────────

In a large bowl, combine the minced red onion, chopped eggs, mayonnaise, Dijon mustard, dillweed, paprika, salt and pepper. Using a fork, mash and stir mixture until well combined.

───────── **She does** ─────────

Place lettuce leaves over bread slices and spoon egg salad over lettuce. Top egg salad with another bread slice to form two sandwiches.

Main
Dishes

Simple
Raisin Oatmeal

1½ C. cold water
⅓ C. raisins
½ tsp. salt

½ tsp. cinnamon
⅔ C. quick cooking oats

She does

In a medium saucepan over medium heat, combine cold water, raisins, salt and cinnamon. Bring mixture to a boil.

He does

Stir in quick cooking oats, reduce heat and let simmer for 1 minute, stirring often. Remove saucepan from heat, cover and let stand for 5 minutes.

Wild Rice Quiche

½ small onion
½ small red bell pepper
½ lb. smoked turkey
1 (10″) unbaked pie shell
2 T. butter
2 C. shredded Swiss cheese

1 C. prepared wild rice
4 eggs
1 C. half n' half
½ tsp. salt
1 T. Worcestershire sauce

──────── She does ────────

Preheat oven to 425°. Chop the onion and the red bell pepper.

──────── He does ────────

Dice the smoked turkey. Place unbaked pie shell in a glass quiche pan.

──────── She does ────────

In a medium saucepan over medium heat, sauté chopped onions and chopped red bell peppers in butter, heating until onions are transparent.

──────── He does ────────

In pie shell, spread diced turkey in an even layer. Spread sautéed onions and peppers over turkey and top with shredded Swiss cheese and prepared wild rice.

──────── She does ────────

In a blender, combine eggs, half n' half, salt and Worcestershire sauce at high speed for 30 seconds. Immediately pour mixture over ingredients in pie shell. Bake in oven for 15 minutes. Reduce heat to 325° and continue baking for an additional 30 minutes. Remove from oven and allow to rest 15 minutes before cutting into wedges. Serve warm.

Baked Breakfast Ramekins

1 clove garlic
1 small tomato
2 strips bacon

1 T. dried onion flakes
2 eggs
Salt and pepper to taste

She does
Preheat oven to 325°. Mince the garlic and dice the tomato.

He does
In a medium skillet over medium high heat, cook the bacon strips until crispy. Remove bacon to paper towels to drain. Crumble bacon into small pieces and set aside. Drain fat from skillet.

She does
In same skillet over medium heat, combine minced garlic, diced tomatoes and dried onion flakes. Sauté until thoroughly heated and stir in crumbled bacon.

He does
Divide mixture evenly into two small ramekins. Carefully crack 1 egg over mixture in each ramekin. Sprinkle salt and pepper over egg and carefully place in oven for 20 to 25 minutes.

Gingerbread Waffles

3 eggs, separated
1 C. skim milk
½ C. dark molasses
½ C. brown sugar
1¾ C. flour
4 tsp. baking powder

½ tsp. salt, optional
1 tsp. cinnamon
1 tsp. ground ginger
¼ tsp. ground cloves
½ C. butter

———————— He does ————————

Preheat and lightly grease a waffle iron. In a medium bowl, beat egg yolks with a whisk. Stir in milk, molasses and brown sugar, mixing until blended.

———————— She does ————————

Into a separate bowl, sift flour, baking powder, salt, cinnamon, ground ginger and ground cloves. In a small glass measuring cup, melt butter in microwave.

———————— He does ————————

Alternating, add melted butter and flour mixture to molasses mixture, mixing slightly.

———————— She does ————————

In a medium mixing bowl, beat egg whites at medium high speed until stiff peaks form. Fold egg whites into batter. Pour about ½ cup batter at a time onto the preheated waffle iron to cook. Repeat with remaining batter.

Chicken Cacciatore

1 small onion
2 T. flour
¾ tsp. salt
2 chicken breasts
2 T. vegetable oil
1 (8 oz.) can tomato sauce

⅓ C. water
1 bay leaf
¼ tsp. dried oregano
½ tsp. dried basil
⅛ tsp. garlic powder
⅛ tsp. pepper

She does

Cut the onion into thin slices.

He does

In a medium bowl, combine flour and salt. Dredge chicken breasts in flour mixture until evenly coated.

She does

In a large skillet over medium heat, place vegetable oil. Add chicken and heat until browned on both sides, turning once. Remove chicken from skillet and set on a plate, covering to keep warm.

He does

Add onion slices to skillet and sauté until tender. Return chicken to skillet and add tomato sauce, water, bay leaf, dried oregano, dried basil, garlic powder and pepper. Stir lightly until well combined. Cover skillet and let simmer for 25 minutes, or until chicken is thoroughly cooked.

Turkey
Broccoli Delight

**1 (10 oz.) pkg. frozen
chopped broccoli**
4 oz. cooked turkey
1 (10½ oz.) can chicken gravy

1 egg
½ tsp. salt
3 T. grated Parmesan cheese

--------------------- **He does** ---------------------

Preheat oven to 375°. Bring a medium pot filled with lightly salted water to a boil over medium heat. Add chopped broccoli and cook until broccoli is tender, about 10 minutes. Drain water from pot and transfer cooked broccoli to an 8" square baking dish.

--------------------- **She does** ---------------------

Dice the cooked turkey into small pieces. Sprinkle diced turkey over broccoli and pour gravy over turkey in baking dish.

--------------------- **He does** ---------------------

In a small bowl, combine egg and salt. Fold in grated Parmesan cheese and spoon mixture over ingredients in baking dish. Bake in oven for 10 minutes.

Chicken in Curry Sauce

½ small onion
2 chicken breast halves
¼ tsp. seasoned salt
¼ tsp. paprika

⅔ C. plus 2 T. water, divided
1 chicken bouillon cube
¼ tsp. curry powder
1 T. flour

She does

Preheat oven to 350°. Mince the onion.

He does

Season chicken breast halves on both sides with seasoned salt and paprika. Place seasoned chicken in an 8″ square baking dish.

She does

In a small saucepan over high heat, bring ⅔ cup water to a boil. Stir in chicken bouillon, mixing until bouillon is completely dissolved. Remove from heat and stir in minced onion and curry powder. Pour mixture over chicken in baking dish and cover with aluminum foil. Bake in oven for 30 minutes. After 30 minutes, remove aluminum foil and bake for an additional 45 minutes.

He does

In a large skillet over medium high heat, combine flour and remaining 2 tablespoons cold water. Mix until well combined. Carefully remove chicken from baking dish and place on serving plates. Add liquid from baking dish to flour mixture in skillet. Heat until mixture is bubbly and spoon over chicken on serving plates.

Pepperoni Skillet Pizza

1 (¾ oz.) pkg. yeast
⅓ C. warm water
1½ C. biscuit baking mix
1 T. cornmeal
½ C. shredded mozzarella
   cheese, divided

½ C. tomato sauce
¼ tsp. dried basil
¼ C. grated Parmesan cheese
3 oz. sliced pepperoni

―――――――― She does ――――――――

Preheat oven to 400°. In a small bowl, combine yeast and warm water. Fold in biscuit baking mix, stirring until a soft dough forms. Set aside for 10 minutes.

―――――――― He does ――――――――

Grease an 8″ ovenproof skillet and sprinkle cornmeal over bottom of skillet. Pat dough onto bottom and halfway up sides of skillet. Bake in oven until dough is lightly browned.

―――――――― She does ――――――――

Carefully remove skillet from oven and sprinkle half of the shredded mozzarella cheese over crust.

―――――――― He does ――――――――

In a medium bowl, combine tomato sauce, dried basil and grated Parmesan cheese. Mix until well combined and spread over mozzarella cheese on crust.

―――――――― She does ――――――――

Top pizza with pepperoni slices and remaining shredded mozzarella cheese. Return to oven for an additional 15 minutes.

Swiss Steak & Vegetables

1 tomato	½ tsp. salt
1 small onion	⅛ tsp. pepper
2 stalks celery	1 T. vegetable oil
2 carrots	1 C. water
½ lb. round steak	1 beef bouillon cube
1 T. flour	

She does

Peel and core the tomato. Cut the tomato into wedges. Slice the onion.

He does

Dice the celery and slice the carrots. Cut the round steak into 2 pieces.

She does

In a small bowl, combine flour, salt and pepper. Dredge the steak pieces in the flour mixture until evenly coated.

He does

In a large skillet over medium high heat, place vegetable oil. Once oil is hot, add coated steak pieces to skillet and heat until browned on all sides. Remove skillet from heat and add water and beef bouillon cube to skillet. Return to low heat, stirring often, and let simmer for 35 minutes.

She does

Add tomato wedges, onion slices, diced celery and carrot slices to skillet. Sprinkle additional salt and pepper to taste over vegetables. Cover and let simmer for an additional 15 minutes, or until vegetables are tender.

Italian Spaghetti & Meatballs

½ lb. ground beef
1 tsp. Italian seasoning
2 green onions
½ small green bell pepper
1 T. vegetable oil
1 (15 oz.) can diced tomatoes in juice
½ C. tomato sauce
½ tsp. brown sugar
¼ tsp. dried basil
¼ tsp. dried oregano
¼ tsp. garlic salt
½ (16 oz.) pkg. spaghetti, uncooked
2 T. grated Parmesan cheese

She does

In a medium bowl, combine ground beef and Italian seasoning, working ingredients together with your hands. Shape ground beef into desired sized meatballs.

He does

Chop the green onions and the green bell pepper. In a large skillet over medium high heat, place vegetable oil. Add chopped green onions and chopped green pepper and sauté until vegetables are tender. Stir in tomatoes in juice, tomato sauce, brown sugar, dried basil, dried oregano and garlic salt. Add meatballs as they are ready. Mix until well combined, cover and let simmer for 25 to 30 minutes.

She does

Fill a large pot with lightly salted water and bring to a boil. Add spaghetti and cook for 8 to 10 minutes, or until pasta is al dente. Drain pasta and divide evenly onto serving plates.

He does

Spoon sauce and meatballs over cooked spaghetti on each plate and sprinkle grated Parmesan cheese over each serving.

Swiss Stuffed Pork Chops

2 pork chops
½ C. shredded Swiss cheese
2 T. dried parsley flakes
1¼ tsp. salt, divided
¼ C. dry bread crumbs

Pepper to taste
1 egg
2 T. vegetable oil
1 C. water

He does

Using a sharp knife, carefully cut a 2″ slit lengthwise into one side of each pork chop.

She does

In a medium bowl, combine shredded Swiss cheese, dried parsley flakes and 1 teaspoon salt. Mix until well combined. Stuff mixture into the slit in each pork chop and secure with toothpicks.

He does

In a shallow bowl, combine dry bread crumbs, remaining ¼ teaspoon salt and pepper. Toss lightly. Place egg in a separate shallow bowl and beat lightly with a fork. Dip the stuffed pork chop first into the egg mixture and then into the bread crumb mixture, turning to coat both sides.

She does

In a large skillet over medium high heat, place vegetable oil. Once oil is hot, add pork chops and heat until browned on both sides, turning once. Add water, reduce heat, cover skillet and let simmer for 1 hour.

Simple
Garlic Chicken

1 T. plus 1½ tsp. butter
1 tsp. garlic powder
½ tsp. seasoned salt

½ tsp. onion powder
2 boneless, skinless chicken
breast halves

--- **He does** ---

In a large skillet over medium high heat, melt the butter.

--- **She does** ---

In a small bowl, combine garlic powder, seasoned salt and onion powder. Mix lightly and season chicken breast halves on both sides with garlic powder mixture.

--- **He does** ---

Add seasoned chicken breast halves to skillet and sauté for about 10 to 15 minutes on each side, or until chicken is cooked throughout and juices run clear.

BBQ Spareribs

2 lbs. spareribs
½ small onion
1 clove garlic
1 T. butter
1 T. brown sugar
2 tsp. Worcestershire sauce

1 tsp. dry mustard
2 drops hot pepper sauce
⅓ C. ketchup
2 lemon slices
¼ tsp. salt
Pinch of pepper

He does

Preheat oven to 350°. Cut spareribs into smaller rib sections. Place rib sections in a large skillet or saucepan over medium high heat and add enough water to cover the ribs. Bring water to a boil, reduce heat and let simmer for about 45 minutes.

She does

Chop the onion and mince the garlic.

He does

After 45 minutes, drain water from saucepan. Preheat oven to 350°. Add butter to saucepan. Once butter is melted, stir in brown sugar, Worcestershire sauce, dry mustard, hot pepper sauce, ketchup, lemon slices, salt, pepper, chopped onion and minced garlic. Return pan to medium high heat and bring to a boil for 1 minute. Remove cooked ribs to a 9 x 13″ baking dish and spoon sauce from pan over ribs. Bake in oven for 20 minutes, basting ribs with sauce occasionally.

Lemon Baked Fish Steaks

1 T. lemon juice
⅛ tsp. paprika
⅛ tsp. pepper
¼ tsp. salt

2 fresh or frozen fish
   steaks, thawed
1 T. butter
1 small lemon

She does

In a small bowl, combine lemon juice, paprika, pepper and salt.

He does

Using a pastry brush, brush lemon juice mixture over both sides of fish and place fish in a shallow baking dish. Cover baking dish with aluminum foil and set aside for 30 minutes.

She does

Combine lemon juice, salt, paprika and pepper and brush over both sides of fish. Place fish in a shallow baking dish and cover. Let set for 30 minutes. Meanwhile, cut lemon into wedges.

He does

Preheat oven to 325°. In a small glass measuring cup, melt butter in microwave. Remove aluminum foil from baking dish and pour melted butter over fish and place lemon wedges around fish. Replace aluminum foil over baking dish and bake in oven for 20 to 25 minutes.

Beef Burgundy Filet Mignon

1 clove garlic
2 green onions
1 C. plus 1 tsp. Burgundy or
  other red wine, divided
⅓ C. vegetable oil
⅓ C. soy sauce

½ C. oyster sauce
1½ tsp. dried oregano
2 (6 oz.) fillets filet mignon
2 T. butter, softened
1½ tsp. white pepper

———————— He does ————————

Mince the garlic and green onions.

———————— She does ————————

In a medium saucepan over medium heat, combine minced garlic, 1 cup Burgundy, vegetable oil, soy sauce, oyster sauce and dried oregano. Bring mixture to a boil and remove from heat. Chill sauce mixture in refrigerator for 1 hour.

———————— He does ————————

In an 8″ square baking dish, place filet mignon. Pour chilled sauce over filet mignon and cover tightly with aluminum foil. Return to refrigerator for 4 to 5 hours.

———————— She does ————————

In a small bowl, cream together butter and remaining 1 teaspoon Burgundy. Mix in minced green onions and white pepper, cover tightly and refrigerate.

———————— He does ————————

Preheat grill to high heat and lightly oil the grate. Preheat oven to 200°. Place marinated filet mignon on hot grill and cook to desired doneness, turning once. Remove from grill and place in a clean 8″ square baking dish. Place dollops of the butter mixture over grilled fillets and bake in oven for 2 to 3 minutes, until butter is melted.

Papaya Beef Skewers

½ lb. beef tenderloin
1 small onion
1 small papaya
¼ C. sweet chili sauce
1½ T. Maggi seasoning sauce

1½ T. loose green tea leaves
 or green tea powder
1½ tsp. rice vinegar
1½ tsp. sugar
4 (10″) skewers

He does

Cut the beef tenderloin and onion into 1″ cubes.

She does

Peel and seed the papaya and cut the fruit into 1″ cubes. Reserve the papaya seeds.

He does

In a medium bowl, combine sweet chili sauce, seasoning sauce, green tea leaves, rice vinegar, sugar and 2 teaspoons of the reserved papaya seeds. Mix well and add cubed beef. Toss until evenly coated, cover and chill in refrigerator for 2 hours or overnight.

She does

Preheat grill to medium heat and lightly oil the grate. Slide marinated beef, cubed papaya and cubed onions onto skewers. Place kabobs on grill and heat for 4 to 7 minutes, or until beef is no longer pink and onions are tender.

Chicken in Light Coconut Sauce

½ small onion
½ lb. boneless skinless
  chicken breast halves
1 clove garlic
½ small head cauliflower

1 T. vegetable oil
1 T. yellow curry powder
½ (13½ oz.) can coconut milk
3 T. chicken broth
Salt and pepper to taste

He does

Chop the onion and chicken breast halves into small pieces.

She does

Crush the garlic and chop the head of cauliflower.

He does

In a large skillet over medium heat, heat the vegetable oil. Stir in the chopped onion and crushed garlic. Heat until onions are tender and add chopped chicken. Heat for about 10 minutes, stirring often, until chicken is thoroughly cooked.

She does

Add chopped cauliflower and curry powder to skillet. Slowly mix in coconut milk and chicken broth, stirring constantly. Season with salt and pepper to taste. Reduce heat to low and let simmer, stirring occasionally, for 30 minutes.

Upside-Down Bacon Cheeseburger Pizza

½ onion
½ green bell pepper
2 Roma tomatoes
4 strips bacon
½ lb. ground beef
¾ C. pizza sauce
¼ C. shredded
  Cheddar cheese

1 egg
½ C. milk
1½ tsp. vegetable oil
½ C. flour
⅛ tsp. salt

She does

Chop the the onion, green bell pepper and Roma tomatoes.

He does

Preheat oven to 400°. In a medium skillet over medium high heat, cook the bacon until crispy. Remove bacon to paper towels to drain. Crumble bacon into small pieces and set aside. Drain fat from skillet.

She does

In a large saucepan over medium high heat, sauté the ground beef, chopped onion and chopped green bell pepper until beef is evenly browned. Drain fat from skillet and stir in crumbled bacon and pizza sauce. Spoon mixture into an ungreased 8″ square baking dish. Sprinkle chopped tomatoes and shredded Cheddar cheese over top.

He does

In a medium mixing bowl, slightly beat the egg. Mix in milk and vegetable oil and beat at low speed for 1 minute. Add flour and salt and beat at medium speed for 2 minutes. Pour mixture evenly over the meat in baking dish. Bake in oven for 20 to 30 minutes, or until topping is lightly puffed and golden brown.

Basil Parmesan Noodles

⅓ C. water
1 clove garlic
6 T. butter, divided
1 (3 oz.) pkg. cream
   cheese, softened
Pinch of salt and pepper

3 oz. thin egg noodles
1 T. dried parsley flakes
½ C. grated Parmesan
   cheese, divided
½ tsp. dried basil

─────────────She does─────────────

In a small saucepan over high heat, bring water to a boil. Meanwhile, mince the garlic.

───────────── He does ─────────────

In a medium bowl, combine 2 tablespoons butter, cream cheese, salt and pepper. Mix until well blended. Stir in boiling water, mix well and set aside.

─────────────She does─────────────

Fill a large pot with lightly salted water and bring to a boil. Add egg noodles and cook for 8 to 10 minutes, or until pasta is al dente. Drain pasta and place in a serving bowl.

───────────── He does ─────────────

In a small saucepan over medium heat, melt remaining 4 tablespoons butter. Add minced garlic and sauté until garlic is tender. Pour butter garlic sauce over noodles and toss to mix. Add dried parsley flakes, ½ of the grated Parmesan cheese and dried basil and toss until well combined. Divide noodles onto serving plates and top with cream cheese sauce mixture. Sprinkle remaining grated Parmesan cheese over top.

Mushroom Lime Chicken

4 large mushrooms
1 T. butter
4 T. fresh lime juice, divided
1 T. olive oil, divided

4 chicken breast halves
½ tsp. salt
½ tsp. pepper

He does

Slice the mushrooms. In a small saucepan over medium heat, melt the butter. Add sliced mushrooms and sauté until mushrooms are softened.

She does

Preheat oven broiler. In a small bowl, place 2 tablespoons lime juice and ½ tablespoon olive oil and mix well. Dip each chicken breast half in the lime juice mixture, covering completely. Arrange chicken in an 8″ square baking dish lined with aluminum foil. Sprinkle salt and pepper over chicken. Place baking dish in oven between 6″ and 8″ below broiler. Broil chicken for 15 minutes.

He does

Carefully turn chicken over in baking dish and pour remaining lime juice and olive oil over chicken. Broil for an additional 15 minutes, or until chicken is thoroughly cooked.

She does

Pour sautéed mushrooms over chicken and return to oven to broil for an additional 2 minutes.

Personal Pan Buffalo Chicken Pizzas

2 boneless, skinless chicken
  breast halves
2 T. butter
1 (2 oz.) bottle hot sauce
1 (12 oz.) bottle bleu
  cheese dressing

1 (10 oz.) pkg. of 2 prepared
  personal pizza crusts
1 (8 oz.) pkg. shredded
  mozzarella cheese

--------- **He does** ---------

Preheat oven to 425°. In a large skillet, heat chicken breast halves until chicken is thoroughly cooked, turning once. Remove chicken from skillet and cut into 1″ cubes.

--------- **She does** ---------

In a small glass measuring cup or bowl, melt butter in microwave. In a medium bowl, combine cubed chicken, hot sauce and melted butter. Toss until well combined.

--------- **He does** ---------

Spread bleu cheese dressing over pizza crusts and divide chicken mixture evenly over crust layer. Sprinkle shredded mozzarella cheese over each pizza and bake in oven for 5 to 10 minutes, or until cheese is bubbly and chicken is heated.

Shrimp n' Pasta

2 cloves garlic
6 mushrooms
8 jumbo shrimp
4 oz. spaghetti, uncooked

½ C. butter
½ tsp. salt
½ tsp. pepper
3 T. grated Romano cheese

He does

Mince the garlic and slice the mushrooms. Peel and devein the shrimp.

She does

Fill a large pot with lightly salted water and bring to a boil. Add spaghetti and cook for 8 to 10 minutes, or until pasta is al dente. Drain pasta and set aside.

He does

In a large skillet over medium low heat, melt the butter. Add the minced garlic, sliced mushrooms, peeled shrimp, salt and pepper. Sauté for 5 minutes, stirring occasionally.

She does

Add cooked pasta and grated Romano cheese to skillet and toss until well combined and thoroughly heated. Serve immediately.

Garlic Fried Chicken

2 boneless, skinless chicken breast halves
1 tsp. garlic powder
½ tsp. pepper
½ tsp. salt
½ tsp. paprika

¼ C. seasoned bread crumbs
½ C. flour
¼ C. milk
1 egg
½ C. vegetable oil

She does

Using a meat mallet, pound the chicken breast halves thin.

He does

In a shallow dish, combine the garlic powder, pepper, salt, paprika, bread crumbs and flour.

She does

In a separate shallow dish, whisk together the milk and egg. Dip the chicken breast halves first into the egg mixture and then dredge in the flour mixture, turning to coat both sides.

He does

In a large skillet, place vegetable oil. Heat oil to 350°. Add coated chicken pieces to hot oil and fry for about 5 minutes per side, or until the chicken is thoroughly cooked. Remove chicken from skillet with a slotted spoon and set on paper towels to drain.

Coconut Shrimp

16 large shrimp
1 egg
¾ C. flour, divided
⅔ C. beer

1½ tsp. baking powder
2 C. shredded coconut
1 to 2 C. vegetable oil

―――――――――――― **He does** ――――――――――――
Peel and devein the shrimp, leaving the tails intact.

―――――――――――― **She does** ――――――――――――
In a medium bowl, combine egg, ½ cup flour, beer and baking powder. Cover a baking sheet with waxed paper.

―――――――――――― **He does** ――――――――――――
In a shallow dish, place remaining ¼ cup flour. Place shredded coconut in a separate shallow dish. Holding the shrimp by the tails, dredge first in the flour, shaking off the excess. Then dip shrimp in the beer batter and allow excess to drip off. Next, roll shrimp in the shredded coconut and place on the prepared baking sheet. Place in refrigerator for 30 minutes.

―――――――――――― **She does** ――――――――――――
Meanwhile, in a deep-fryer or skillet, heat vegetable oil to 350°. Add coated shrimp to hot oil in batches and cook for 2 to 3 minutes, or until golden brown, turning once. Use tongs to remove shrimp from hot oil and place on paper towels to drain.

Glazed Avocado Chicken

¼ C. flour
¼ tsp. salt
1 tsp. pepper
1 egg
2 large boneless chicken
   breast halves

2 T. vegetable oil
1 tsp. tarragon
1 tsp. dried basil
1 T. sweet butter
⅔ C. white wine
1 small ripe avocado

He does

In a shallow dish, combine flour, salt and pepper. In a separate dish, place egg and beat slightly. Dip the chicken breast halves first into the beaten egg and then into the flour mixture, turning to coat both sides.

She does

In a medium skillet over high heat, place vegetable oil. Once oil is very hot, add chicken, skin side down, and sauté until golden. Turn chicken over and sauté until tender and thoroughly cooked.

He does

Sprinkle tarragon and dried basil over chicken. Add butter and white wine to skillet and bring to a boil. Reduce heat and let simmer until sauce thickens and becomes glossy.

She does

Peel the avocado and cut into thin strips. Place one cooked chicken breast half on each serving plate. Cover with avocado strips. Pour sauce from skillet evenly over avocado and chicken.

Linguine in Mushroom & Garlic Sauce

3 cloves garlic
3 T. butter
1 (8 oz.) pkg. sliced
   mushrooms
½ tsp. dried rosemary
1 tsp. pepper

½ C. heavy whipping cream
Salt to taste
4 oz. linguine, uncooked
¼ C. shredded
   mozzarella cheese
Fresh chopped parsley

She does

Mince the garlic.

He does

In a large skillet over medium low heat, melt the butter. Stir in the minced garlic, sliced mushrooms, dried rosemary and pepper. Sauté for about 5 to 7 minutes, stirring occasionally. Mix in heavy cream and let simmer for about 3 minutes, or until sauce slightly thickens. Season with salt to taste.

She does

Fill a large pot with lightly salted water and bring to a boil. Add linguine and cook for 8 to 10 minutes, or until pasta is al dente. Drain pasta and stir into sauce mixture in skillet, tossing until well combined. Add shredded mozzarella cheese and toss until cheese begins to melt. Season with fresh parsley and serve.

Penne Pasta Lasagna

8 oz. penne pasta, uncooked
½ lb. ground beef
1 (26 oz.) jar pasta sauce
1 (15 oz.) container grated ricotta cheese

1 C. shredded mozzarella cheese, divided
¼ C. grated Parmesan cheese
1 egg, beaten

She does

Preheat oven to 350°. Grease a 2½ quart baking dish and set aside.

He does

Fill a large pot with lightly salted water and bring to a boil. Add penne pasta and cook for 8 to 10 minutes, or until pasta is al dente.

She does

In a large skillet over medium heat, cook ground beef until browned. Drain fat from skillet. To ground beef in skillet, add pasta sauce. Stir until well combined and remove from heat.

He does

In a medium bowl, combine grated ricotta cheese, shredded mozzarella cheese, grated Parmesan cheese and beaten egg. Stir until well combined.

She does

In the prepared dish, layer half the cooked pasta and top with half of the meat and sauce mixture. Top with half of the cheese mixtures. Repeat layers with remaining pasta, sauce and cheese mixtures. Bake in oven for 35 to 40 minutes, or until lasagna is hot and bubbly.

Hawaiian BBQ Burgers

½ lb. ground beef
¼ C. barbecue sauce
Salt and pepper to taste

2 pineapple rings
4 strips bacon
2 hamburger buns

She does
Preheat grill to medium heat and lightly oil the grate.

He does
In a large bowl, combine ground beef and barbecue sauce, mixing until well combined. Season with salt and pepper to taste and shape mixture into 2 hamburger patties.

She does
Place hamburger patties on grill and cook until heated throughout, turning often. Add pineapple rings to grill during last 5 minutes of cooking time, turning to grill both sides.

He does
In a medium skillet over medium high heat, cook the bacon strips until crispy. Remove bacon to paper towels to drain.

She does
To assemble burgers, place one cooked patty on each hamburger bun and top each with one of the grilled pineapple rings and 2 slices of bacon. If desired, top with additional barbecue sauce and bun tops.

Marmalade Bourbon Pot Roast

¼ C. Dijon mustard
½ tsp. ground red pepper, divided
1 tsp. salt
1 (3 lb.) boneless pork loin roast

1 C. orange marmalade
2 to 3 T. bourbon
2 T. butter

He does

Preheat oven to 325°. In a small bowl, combine Dijon mustard, ¼ teaspoon ground red pepper and salt. Mix well and rub over pork loin. Place roast on a rack in a shallow roasting pan. Roast pork in oven for 1 to 1½ hours, or until roast registers between 155° and 160° on a meat thermometer.

She does

In a small saucepan over low heat, combine orange marmalade, bourbon, butter and remaining ¼ teaspoon ground red pepper. Heat, stirring occasionally, until liquefied but not too runny, about 10 minutes. Remove roast from oven and slice. Drizzle bourbon sauce over sliced roast.

Whiskey Marinated Salmon

1 (½ lb.) fresh salmon filet
1 clove garlic
1 tsp. grated lemon peel
¼ C. lemon juice

¼ C. whiskey
1 T. vegetable oil
¼ tsp. dry mustard
1 T. dried rosemary

─────────────── **She does** ───────────────

Thoroughly rinse salmon and pat dry. Cut filet into 2 pieces. Crush the garlic.

─────────────── **He does** ───────────────

In a shallow dish, combine grated lemon peel, lemon juice, whiskey, vegetable oil, dry mustard, dried rosemary and crushed garlic. Set aside half of the marinade mixture. Add salmon pieces and turn until coated in remaining marinade mixture. Cover and let marinate in refrigerator for 1 to 1½ hours.

─────────────── **She does** ───────────────

Remove salmon from refrigerator and drain. Preheat broiler. Place salmon pieces on a broiler pan and brush with reserved marinade mixture and sprinkle with dried rosemary. Place salmon 4″ under broiler for 5 minutes. Turn salmon over and brush with additional marinade. Place under broiler for 5 more minutes. Salmon is done when it flakes easily with a fork.

Italian Baked Orange Roughy

¼ C. butter
¼ C. Italian seasoned dry
   bread crumbs
2 T. grated Parmesan cheese
2 T. grated Romano cheese

¼ tsp. garlic powder
½ tsp. salt
1 lb. orange roughy filets
1 T. fresh chopped parsley

He does

Preheat oven to 400°. Lightly grease a medium baking dish and set aside. In a small glass measuring cup, melt butter in microwave.

She does

In a shallow bowl, combine bread crumbs, grated Parmesan cheese, grated Romano cheese, garlic powder and salt. Brush both sides of orange roughy filets with melted butter and dredge filets in the bread crumb mixture. Arrange filets in a single layer in the prepared baking dish and sprinkle with fresh parsley. Bake in oven for 10 to 15 minutes, or until fish flakes easily with a fork. Serve warm.

Artichoke Chicken

1 small onion
4 mushrooms
1 T. butter or margarine
4 boneless, skinless chicken
   breast halves
1 (6 oz.) jar marinated
   artichoke hearts, drained

2½ T. flour
1 tsp. dried rosemary
½ tsp. salt
¼ tsp. pepper
½ C. chicken broth
½ C. dry white wine

He does

Chop the onion and slice the mushrooms.

She does

In a large skillet over medium heat, place butter. When butter is melted, add chicken breast halves to skillet and cook, turning once to brown both sides. Transfer browned chicken to a greased 9 x 13″ baking dish. Place drained artichoke hearts and sliced mushrooms over chicken.

He does

Preheat oven to 350°. In same skillet, sauté chopped onions until softened. Mix in flour, dried rosemary, salt and pepper, mixing until smooth. Gradually stir in chicken broth and dry white wine. Heat until sauce is thickened and bubbly. Remove sauce from heat and spoon over chicken in baking dish.

She does

Cover baking dish with aluminum foil and bake in oven for 50 to 60 minutes, or until chicken is thoroughly cooked.

Chicken Stir-Fry

4 boneless skinless chicken
   breast halves
2 stalks celery
1 large carrot
1 small onion
3 T. cornstarch
2 T. soy sauce
½ tsp. ground ginger
¼ tsp. garlic powder

3 T. vegetable oil, divided
2 C. frozen broccoli florets
1 C. water
1 tsp. chicken
   bouillon granules
⅔ C. shortening, softened
1 egg
1 tsp. vanilla
½ C. buttermilk

He does

Cut the chicken into ½″ strips.

She does

Chop the celery and carrot and cut the onion into wedges.

He does

In a large ziplock bag, place chicken strips. Add cornstarch. Seal bag and toss until chicken is coated. In a small bowl, combine soy sauce, ground ginger and garlic powder. Add mixture to ziplock bag. Seal bag and shake well. Place filled bag in refrigerator for 30 minutes.

She does

In a large skillet or wok over high heat, place 2 tablespoons vegetable oil. Add coated chicken from bag. Discard bag and any remaining seasoning. Stir-fry chicken until no longer pink, about 3 to 5 minutes. Remove chicken from skillet and keep warm.

He does

Add broccoli florets, chopped celery, chopped carrots and onion wedges to skillet and stir fry for 4 to 5 minutes, or until tender but still crisp. Add water and chicken bouillon granules to skillet with vegetables. Return chicken to skillet and heat until liquid is thick and bubbly.

Southwestern Meatloaf

1 C. cornflakes
1 small green bell pepper
1 (1 oz.) env. onion soup mix
1 lb. ground beef
1 C. whole kernel corn

2 eggs
¾ C. water
⅓ C. ketchup
½ C. salsa

She does

Preheat oven to 350°. Crush the cornflakes and chop the green bell pepper.

He does

In a large bowl, combine crushed cornflakes, chopped green bell pepper, onion soup mix, ground beef, whole kernel corn, eggs, water and ketchup. Mix by hand until well combined. Press mixture into a 5 x 9″ loaf pan. Bake, uncovered, in oven for 1 hour, or until thoroughly cooked.

She does

Carefully remove meatloaf from oven and let stand for 10 minutes. Before serving, pour salsa over top of meatloaf and spread evenly.

Basil Stuffed Chicken

1 T. olive oil
1 small tomato
4 boneless, skinless chicken
  breast halves
½ tsp. salt
½ tsp. pepper

4 slices mozzarella cheese
4 fresh basil leaves
½ C. seasoned bread crumbs
1 T. grated Parmesan cheese
1 T. mayonnaise

He does

Preheat oven broiler and grease the broiler pan with olive oil. Place broiler pan 8″ below heat. Cut 4 slices from the tomato.

She does

Place chicken breast halves between two sheets of plastic wrap. Using a meat mallet, lightly pound the chicken breast halves and season chicken with salt and pepper. Using a sharp knife, cut each chicken breast half horizontally almost in half, but leaving one side still attached. Place 1 mozzarella cheese slice, 1 tomato slice and 1 basil leaf inside each chicken breast half and press to enclose the filling.

He does

In a shallow bowl, combine seasoned bread crumbs and grated Parmesan cheese, mixing until well combined. Use a pastry brush to brush mayonnaise over each chicken breast half and dip each in the bread crumb mixture, turning to coat both sides.

She does

Lightly coat both sides of chicken with non-stick cooking spray and place on prepared broiler pan. Broil for 8 to 10 minutes, turning once, or until chicken registers 170° on a meat thermometer.

Salmon in Portabella Sauce

1 large king salmon filet
1 portabella mushroom
4 green onions
½ T. olive oil

1 tsp. tarragon
½ C. white wine
1 C. sour cream

——————————— He does ———————————

Preheat oven to 375°. In a large oven-safe pan, place salmon filet skin-side down. Bake for 1 hour, until salmon is light orange in color.

——————————— She does ———————————

Slice the portabella mushroom and chop the green onions. In a large skillet over low heat, heat olive oil. Add sliced mushrooms, chopped green onions, tarragon and white wine and sauté until cooked throughout. About 5 to 10 minutes before serving, add sour cream and stir until heated.

——————————— He does ———————————

Remove salmon from oven and place on serving dish. Pour mushroom mixture over salmon filets. Serve immediately.

Simply Chic
Seafood Bisque

¼ lb. fresh shrimp
½ lb. white fish
½ C. chicken or
   vegetable broth
¼ lb. fresh or
   imitation crabmeat
4 C. tomato soup

1½ T. curry
2 C. evaporated milk
3 T. fresh lemon juice
1 tsp. nutmeg
Lemon slices and dried
   parsley flakes, optional

She does

Peel and devein the shrimp.

He does

In a large skillet over medium high heat, lightly sauté white fish in broth. Add peeled shrimp and heat until shrimp turn pink.

She does

In a large non-aluminum pot, combine sautéed white fish, cooked shrimp, crabmeat, tomato soup, curry, evaporated milk, lemon juice and nutmeg. Mix lightly and place pot over medium heat. Heat until soup is slightly steaming, being careful not to boil. Can be served either hot or chilled. If desired, garnish with lemon slices and a pinch of dried parsley flakes.

Desserts

Chocolate Cheesecakes for Two

1 (1 oz.) square semi-sweet
  baking chocolate
1 (3 oz. pkg.) cream
  cheese, softened

1 T. sugar
½ C. frozen whipped
  topping, thawed
2 chocolate sandwich cookies

--------- He does ---------

In a double boiler over simmering water, heat the semi-sweet chocolate square, stirring occasionally, until completely melted.

---------She does---------

In a medium bowl, use a wire whisk to beat together cream cheese, sugar and melted chocolate. Fold in whipped topping and mix well.

--------- He does ---------

Place 1 chocolate sandwich cookie in the bottom of each of 2 large muffin cups filled with paper liners. Pour cream cheese mixture over cookie in each cup. Chill in refrigerator at least 2 hours or place in freezer for 1 hour.

Brown Sugar & Walnut Baked Apples

2 large baking apples
1 T. chopped walnuts
2 T. raisins

3 T. brown sugar, divided
¼ tsp. cinnamon
¼ C. water

―――――――――――**She does**―――――――――――

Preheat oven to 400°. Core apples and place in a small baking dish.

―――――――――――**He does**―――――――――――

In a medium bowl, combine chopped walnuts, raisins, 1 tablespoon brown sugar and cinnamon. Mix well and divide mixture evenly into hollowed part of each apple.

―――――――――――**She does**―――――――――――

In a separate bowl, combine water and remaining 2 tablespoons brown sugar. Mix well and pour over apples in baking dish. Cover baking dish with aluminum foil and bake in oven for 40 to 45 minutes.

Mini
Apple Pies

1 tart apple
¼ C. plus 1 T. sugar
¼ tsp. cinnamon

3 T. flour
1½ T. butter or margarine
2 mini unbaked pastry shells

He does

Preheat oven to 400°. Slice the apple. In a medium bowl, combine sliced apples, ¼ cup sugar and cinnamon. Toss until well combined and divide evenly into pastry shells.

She does

In a small bowl, combine remaining 1 tablespoon sugar, flour and butter, mixing until coarse crumbs form. Sprinkle mixture over apples in pastry shells. Bake in oven for 35 to 40 minutes.

Peach Cobbler Cups

1 large peach
2 tsp. cornstarch
3 T. brown sugar
¼ C. cold water
1 T. butter or margarine

1 tsp. lemon juice
2 refrigerated flakey
   biscuits, unbaked
Coarse sugar

She does

Preheat oven to 400°. Slice the peach.

He does

In a medium saucepan over medium heat, combine cornstarch, brown sugar and cold water. Mix until combined and stir in sliced peaches. Continue to heat, stirring occasionally, until mixture is bubbly. Stir in butter and lemon juice, mixing until butter is melted. Divide mixture evenly into 2 oven-safe custard cups or small ramekins.

She does

Place one of the unbaked refrigerated biscuit over peaches in each ramekin. Sprinkle coarse sugar over top and bake in oven for 25 minutes.

Fruit n' Dumplings

1 (8½ oz.) can fruit cocktail
½ (11 oz.) can mandarin
  orange slices
3 T. sugar, divided
1 tsp. butter or margarine
2 tsp. lemon juice
½ C. flour

1 tsp. baking powder
¼ tsp. salt
1 T. sugar
¼ C. milk
1 tsp. vegetable oil
⅛ tsp. cinnamon

He does

In a medium saucepan over medium high heat, combine fruit cocktail in juice, mandarin orange slices, 2 tablespoons sugar, butter and lemon juice. Bring mixture to a boil, stirring often.

She does

Into a medium bowl, sift the flour, baking powder, salt and remaining 1 tablespoon sugar. Stir in milk and vegetable oil. Mix until a light batter forms.

He does

Drop tablespoonfuls of batter over boiling fruit mixture in saucepan. Sprinkle cinnamon over batter. Cover saucepan and cook over medium heat for 10 to 12 minutes, or until dumplings are golden brown.

Raspberry Crème

1½ C. fresh raspberries
1 T. sugar
1 C. raspberry ice cream

¼ C. sour cream
1 T. orange liqueur

She does

Place raspberries in a medium bowl and sprinkle sugar over berries. Toss lightly and place in refrigerator until chilled.

He does

Once berries are chilled, fold in raspberry ice cream, sour cream and orange liqueur, mixing until well combined. Place in freezer for 1 hour. To serve, divide mixture evenly into 2 dessert dishes.

Fluffy Java Parfaits

1½ C. miniature
   marshmallows
½ C. water
1 tsp. instant coffee granules

1 C. frozen whipped
   cream, thawed
½ C. chocolate wafer crumbs

He does

In a medium saucepan over medium low heat, combine minia-ture marshmallows, water and instant coffee granules. Heat, stirring often, until marshmallows are completely melted.

She does

Remove from heat and let cool until partially set. Fold in whipped cream. To assemble parfaits, in two dessert glasses, alter-nate layers of the marshmallow mixture and the chocolate wafer crumbs, forming two or three layers in each glass.

Taffy Molasses Bars

½ C. brown sugar
⅓ C. shortening
¼ C. molasses
1 egg
1¼ C. flour

½ tsp. baking powder
¼ tsp. baking soda
⅛ tsp. salt
¼ C. chopped nuts, optional

She does

Preheat oven to 350°. In a medium saucepan over medium heat, combine brown sugar, shortening and molasses. Heat, stirring often, until shortening melts. Remove from heat and let cool slightly.

He does

In a medium mixing bowl, beat egg. Add molasses mixture and beat until light and fluffy.

She does

Into a separate bowl, sift the flour, baking powder, baking soda and salt. Add to fluffy mixture and blend well. Spread mixture into a well greased 8″ square baking dish. If desired, sprinkle chopped nuts over top and bake in oven for 15 to 18 minutes.

Light Lemon Sauce

¼ C. sugar
2 tsp. cornstarch
⅛ tsp. salt
⅛ tsp. nutmeg
½ C. cold water

1 egg yolk
1 T. butter or margarine
½ tsp. grated lemon peel
1 T. lemon juice

―――――――――――― He does ――――――――――――

In a medium saucepan over low heat, combine sugar, cornstarch, salt and nutmeg. Stir in cold water. Heat, stirring occasionally, until mixture is thick and bubbly.

―――――――――――― She does ――――――――――――

In a separate bowl, beat egg yolk lightly with a fork. Stir a small amount of the hot sugar mixture into egg yolk. Mix well and return all to the hot mixture in saucepan. Heat and stir for 1 minute.

―――――――――――― He does ――――――――――――

Remove from heat and fold in grated lemon peel and lemon juice. Mix until well blended. Use Lemon Sauce as a topping for angel food cake, white cake or vanilla cupcakes.

Chocolate Brownie Cookies

5 (1 oz.) squares bittersweet
    baking chocolate
2 (1 oz.) squares unsweetened
    baking chocolate
¼ C. flour
¼ tsp. baking powder
⅛ tsp. salt

2 large eggs
⅔ C. sugar
½ T. brewed espresso
1 tsp. vanilla
2 T. butter
¾ C. mini chocolate chips

She does

Preheat oven to 375°. Line two baking sheets with parchment paper. Coarsely chop the bittersweet and unsweetened baking chocolate.

He does

In a small bowl, whisk together the flour, baking powder and salt. Mix well and set aside.

She does

In a medium mixing bowl, lightly whip the eggs. Add the sugar, brewed espresso and vanilla and beat at high speed for about 5 minutes, until thickened.

He does

In a double boiler over simmering heat, place the butter. Stir in chopped bittersweet chocolate and chopped unsweetened chocolate, mixing until chocolate is completely melted. Gently fold the melted chocolate mixture into the egg mixture. Add flour mixture and mix slowly. Fold in the chocolate chips. If batter is runny, let it sit for about 5 minutes, until slightly thickened.

She does

Drop teaspoonfuls of the batter onto the prepared baking sheets. Bake in oven for 8 to 9 minutes, or until cookies are puffed and slightly cracked.

Strawberry Shortcake

1 (8 oz.) pkg. strawberries
1 T. sugar
½ C. flour
¾ tsp. baking powder
⅛ tsp. cream of tartar

⅛ tsp. baking soda
2 T. butter or margarine
¼ C. buttermilk
¾ C. whipped cream
Coarse sugar

She does

Hull and slice the strawberries.

He does

Preheat oven to 400°. Grease a baking sheet and set aside.

She does

In a medium bowl, combine sliced strawberries and sugar. Mix lightly and set aside.

He does

In a medium mixing bowl, combine flour, baking powder, cream of tartar and baking soda. Using a pastry blender, cut in the butter until mixture resembles coarse crumbs. Form a well in the center of the dry ingredients and add buttermilk to well. Using a fork, stir just until moistened.

She does

Drop dough into 2 mounds onto the prepared baking sheet. Sprinkle coarse sugar over biscuits. Bake in oven for 10 to 12 minutes, or until biscuits are golden.

He does

Remove biscuits from oven and split each one open on a plate. Spoon some of the sliced strawberries and whipped topping over the bottom half of each biscuit. Add the top half of each biscuit and top with additional sliced strawberries and whipped topping.

Glazed Lemon Bars

1½ C. plus 2 T. biscuit
   baking mix, divided
¾ C. plus 3 T. powdered
   sugar, divided
5 T. butter or margarine

1½ C. sugar
1 T. grated lemon peel
¼ C. plus 1½ T. lemon
   juice, divided
4 eggs

She does

Preheat oven to 350°. In a medium bowl, combine 1½ cups baking mix and 3 tablespoons powdered sugar. Using a pastry blender, cut in butter until mixture is crumbly. Press mixture into the bottom of an ungreased 9 x 13″ baking dish. Bake in oven for 10 minutes, until light brown.

He does

In a separate bowl, combine sugar, remaining 2 tablespoons baking mix, grated lemon peel, ¼ cup lemon juice and eggs. Pour mixture over crust layer in baking dish. Return to oven for an additional 25 minutes, or until center is set. While still warm, loosen edges from sides of pan.

She does

In a small bowl, combine remaining ¾ cup powdered sugar and remaining 1½ tablespoons lemon juice. Mix until smooth. Spread mixture over baked lemon bars. Let cool completely before cutting into bars.

Apple Strudel

2 lbs. apples
½ C. sugar
1 tsp. cinnamon
⅔ C. raisins

2 T. rum
½ C. pine nuts or hazelnuts
1 sheet puff pastry
1 to 2 egg yolks, beaten

She does

Preheat oven to 375°. Peel, core and chop the apples.

He does

In a large saucepan over low heat, combine chopped apples, sugar, cinnamon, raisins, rum and nuts. Let mixture steep until apples have softened.

She does

Roll out puff pastry on a flat, lightly floured cloth. Stretch out pastry with hands until paper thin. Trim edges of pastry if they are thick or uneven. Pour apple mixture over pastry and spread evenly. Lift side of cloth little by little until puff pastry rolls up and over filling. Transfer strudel to a lightly greased baking sheet and press edges of pastry together along sides.

He does

In a small bowl, beat the egg yolks and brush over pastry. Bake in oven for 30 minutes, or until pastry is browned and crisp. To serve, cut strudel into slices and serve with vanilla sauce or over vanilla ice cream.

Rhubarb Cake

4 to 5 stalks rhubarb
1 C. margarine, softened
3 C. brown sugar
2 eggs
2 C. buttermilk
2 tsp. baking soda

1 tsp. salt
1 tsp. vanilla
4 C. flour
1 C. sugar
2 tsp. cinnamon

He does

Preheat oven to 350°. Chop the rhubarb.

She does

In a large bowl, combine softened margarine, brown sugar, eggs and buttermilk. Mix in baking soda, salt, vanilla, flour and chopped rhubarb. Stir until evenly blended. Pour mixture into a greased 11 x 15″ baking dish.

He does

In a small bowl, combine sugar and cinnamon. Sprinkle mixture over ingredients in baking dish. Bake in oven for 40 minutes.

Chocolate Raspberry Truffles

8 (1 oz.) squares semi-sweet
   baking chocolate
2½ C. crushed
   chocolate wafers
1 C. ground almonds

¾ C. powdered sugar
½ C. raspberry preserves
⅓ C. coffee-flavored liqueur
4 (1 oz.) squares
   white chocolate

He does

Coarsely chop the baking chocolate. In a double boiler over simmering water, place the chopped baking chocolate. Heat, stirring often, until completely melted.

She does

In a medium bowl, combine crushed chocolate wafers, ground almonds and powdered sugar. Mix well and blend in melted semi-sweet chocolate, raspberry preserves and coffee liqueur. Shape mixture into 1″ balls. Place balls on a baking sheet and chill in refrigerator for 15 minutes.

He does

Coarsely chop the white chocolate. In a double boiler over simmering water, place chopped white chocolate. Heat until chocolate is completely melted. Quickly dip chilled chocolate balls in white chocolate and return to baking sheet. Chill in refrigerator until white chocolate is hardened.

Pumpkin Pie Cake

1 (30 oz.) can pumpkin puree
1 (12 oz.) can
  evaporated milk
3 eggs
1¼ C. sugar
1 tsp. allspice
¾ tsp. ground ginger

2 tsp. cinnamon
½ tsp. salt
1 (18 oz.) pkg. yellow
  cake mix
¾ C. butter
1 C. chopped nuts

────────── She does ──────────

Preheat oven to 350°. In a large bowl, combine pumpkin puree, evaporated milk, eggs, sugar, allspice, ground ginger, cinnamon and salt. Mix well and pour mixture into a greased 9 x 13″ baking dish.

────────── He does ──────────

In a small glass measuring cup, melt butter in microwave. Sprinkle dry yellow cake mix over pumpkin mixture and gently pat down. Sprinkle chopped nuts over cake mix in pan. Drizzle melted butter over ingredients in pan. Bake in oven for 50 minutes. Remove cake from oven and let cool slightly before cutting into squares.

Mango Shortbread

1 mango
1½ C. butter
¾ C. sugar, divided

3¼ C. flour, divided
1½ tsp. cinnamon
Pinch of nutmeg

—————————————She does—————————————

Peel and seed the mango. Chop the mango flesh.

————————————— He does —————————————

Preheat oven to 350°. In a large bowl, cream together butter and ½ cup sugar. Sift 3 cups flour into the butter mixture and mix well. Press ½ of the mixture into the bottom of a 9 x 13″ baking dish.

—————————————She does—————————————

In a medium bowl, combine chopped mango, remaining ¼ cup sugar, remaining ¼ cup flour, cinnamon and nutmeg. Toss all together until well combined. Pour mixture over crust layer in baking dish.

————————————— He does —————————————

Sprinkle the remaining butter mixture over the mango filling and press down lightly. Bake in oven for 1 hour, or until topping is golden brown. Remove from oven and let cool for 15 minutes before cutting into bars.

Bananas Foster

3 bananas
¼ C. butter
⅔ C. dark brown sugar
3½ T. dark rum

1½ tsp. vanilla
½ tsp. cinnamon
¼ C. chopped walnuts
1 pint vanilla ice cream

─────────── He does ───────────

Peel the bananas. Cut each banana in half and slice the halves lengthwise.

─────────── She does ───────────

In a large skillet over medium heat, melt the butter. Stir in the dark brown sugar, rum, vanilla and cinnamon. Heat until mixture begins to bubble. Add sliced bananas and chopped walnuts to the skillet. Heat until bananas are hot, about 1 to 2 minutes.

─────────── He does ───────────

Scoop desired amount of vanilla ice cream into two serving bowls. Pour the bananas and sauce over ice cream and serve immediately.

Strawberry Chilled Dessert Soup

**1 (16 oz.) pkg. fresh
   strawberries**
2 C. milk

1 C. heavy whipping cream
½ C. sour cream
Sugar to taste

She does

Hull and coarsely chop the strawberries.

He does

In a blender, combine chopped strawberries, milk, heavy cream and sour cream. Process on high until well blended and smooth. Transfer blended mixture to a medium bowl.

She does

Stir in sugar to taste and cover bowl with plastic wrap. Chill in refrigerator for 8 hours or overnight.

Index

Soups & Sandwiches

Main Dishes

—————————— Desserts ——————————